Reform
and
Renewal

A festival service celebrating
the renewal of the church over the centuries

compiled by
Michael Hampel, Andrew Reid and Tim Ruffer

RS✦M

RS◆M

The Royal School of Church Music
19 The Close, Salisbury, Wiltshire, SP1 2EB, England
Tel: +44 (0)1722 424848 Fax: +44 (0)1722 424849
Email: press@rscm.com Website: www.rscm.com
Registered charity 312828

Reform
and
Renewal

RSCM Catalogue Number: RS51
RSCM Music Direct Order Code: S0173
ISBN: 978-0-85402-258-8

Cover design by Anthony Marks
Cover image: Martin Luther preaching, detail from the altarpiece of the Church of Torslunde,
1561 (tempera on panel), Dutch School, (16th century) / Nationalmuseet, Copenhagen,
Denmark / De Agostini Picture Library / A. Dagli Orti / Bridgeman Images
Music setting by Ashley Harries and RSCM Press
With thanks to Daniel Soper
Printed in Great Britain by Halstan & Co, Amersham, UK.

Contents

Pastoral Introduction

In 2017, we mark the five hundredth anniversary of the nailing by Martin Luther to a church door in Wittenburg his '95 theses' which articulated his objections to certain Church practices – practices which he saw as corrupting the Church of God's dear Son Jesus Christ. Thus was sparked a series of controversies, debates, political manoeuvring, reform and counter reform known collectively as 'The Reformation', followed swiftly by Counter Reformation. Churches broke away from the authority of the Church of Rome and the Pope and formed new enclaves in which liturgy and music in particular – not to mention the reading of the Word of God in the Bible – were transformed into new styles of worship usually in the mother tongue of worshippers.

Since then, revision and regrouping have been hallmarks of the development of the Church – changes which have co-existed, for better or for worse, alongside greater attempts at ecumenical dialogue and moves towards unity in diversity.

This RSCM Festival Service Book marks this special anniversary and celebrates unity in diversity with music from across the centuries and reference to significant moments in which change has occurred and liturgy has developed. It is not a celebration of one style over another or of one form over another but, instead, seeks to exploit in the best sense the resources which Reformation has bequeathed to us, while also encouraging us to look forward to all that is yet to be revealed to us by God in Christ.

Michael Hampel
Precentor, St Paul's Cathedral, London

Using the book

There are at least two options for all the musical items in this service. With the hymns, there is a choice between traditional hymnody, and worship songs or contemporary hymns. When making your choice, it might be worth considering a mix of old and new. We have also provided choral items suitable for full SATB choirs and those with more limited resources. Equally suitable for Area Festivals performed by hundreds and for smaller local services, *Reform and Renewal* provides invaluable resources for churches of all sizes.

The service is through composed. Should you choose the first musical option, at the end of that item there is guidance for where to pick up the service, missing out the musical item you won't be using.

The book also provides resources so that it may be adapted for use at Choral Evensong, and guidance for using the book under those circumstances can be found on page viii.

Some Area Festivals feature music that *Voice for Life* award winners can sing. We have provided a number of opportunities for this:

> Greater love by John Ireland: bars 55–65;
>
> Let the word of Christ by Richard Shephard: bars 67–74
>
> I give to you a new commandment by Peter Nardone: bars 4–20

and if using the Sarum Service Magnificat & Nunc dimittis by Malcolm Archer:

> Magnificat bars 38–45,
>
> Nunc dimittis bars 3–11.

Additionally, a verse of a hymn could be sung by award winners alone.

A congregational service leaflet can be found on the RSCM website: www.rscmshop.com/s0173.html

Please note that words of the hymns in copyright require a CCLI licence to reproduce in a service leaflet.

Andrew Reid & Tim Ruffer
RSCM

OUTLINE OF THE SERVICE

THE GATHERING

PRAYERS OF PENITENCE

THE WORD OF GOD

ADDITIONAL CHORAL RESOURCES

Suggested Order of Service for Choral Evensong

Reform
and
Renewal

¶ THE GATHERING

Opening Hymn: A mighty fortress is our God

Words: *Ein Feste Burg ist unser Gott*
MARTIN LUTHER (1483–1546)
translated by FREDERICK HENRY HEDGE (1805–1890)

Melody: MARTIN LUTHER (1483–1546)
Verses 1, 3 and 4 arranged: JOHN RUTTER
verse 2 harmonized: J. S. BACH

VERSE 1 (Choir and congregation)

1. A migh - ty for - tress is our God, A

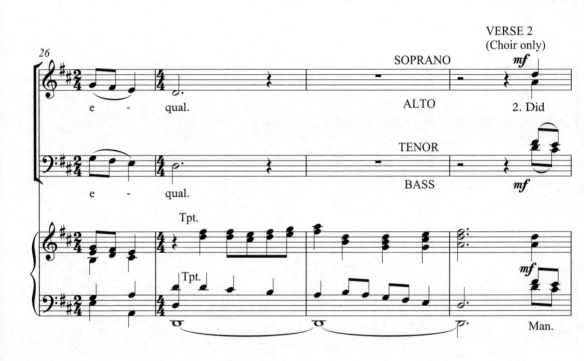

(Organ doubling choir)

los - ing; Were not_ the_ right_ man_ on_ our_ side, The

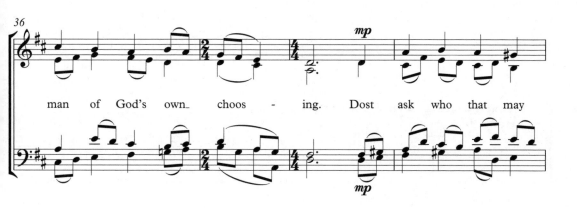

man of God's own_ choos - ing. Dost ask who that may

be? Christ Je - sus, it is he; Lord

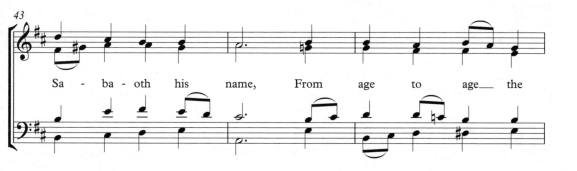

Sa - ba - oth his name, From age to age_ the

same, And he must win the___ bat - tle.

TENORS and BASSES

VERSE 3 (Choir and congregation)

unis.

3. And though this world, with de - vils filled, Should

Sw. reeds

Tpt.

SOPRANOS and ALTOS

unis.

We will not fear,___ for

threat-en to un - do___ us,

Gt.

Ped.

One lit - tle word shall fell____ him.

sure;

-32'

VERSE 4
(Choir and cong.)

ALL VOICES   *f*

4. That

word a - bove_ all earth - ly pow'rs, No thanks to them, a - bid -

bo - dy they may__ kill;   God's   truth__ a - bid - deth

still;   His   king - dom__ is   for - ev - er.

For Choral Evensong, turn to page 138

Bidding Prayer

We are gathered here today in the five hundredth year since Martin Luther presented the Church with his writings objecting to certain church practices, writings which saw the dawn of reformation in the Church.

We give thanks to God for reform and renewal, for opportunities to preach the Gospel afresh in each generation, and for the privilege of worshipping God in the beauty of holiness; for tradition and innovation, for courage and obedience, for unity in diversity.

And, as we give thanks for our inheritance of the Faith at the hands of holy men and women in the past, so we pray today for peace in the Church: that all may worship the one true God, Father, Son and Holy Spirit, and that all may be one as Christ is one with his Church.

And, as we pray, so also we remember all who need our prayers: the poor and the unloved, the lonely and the fearful, the sick and the bereaved; and all who find it difficult to live at unity with others; that Christ's healing touch may be laid upon them and his sustaining presence be with them.

All these our thoughts and prayers, let us offer up to the throne of God in the words our Saviour Christ commanded and taught us, praying:

**Our Father,
who art in heaven;
hallowed be thy name.
Thy Kingdom come,
thy will be done on earth as it is in heaven.
Give us this day our daily bread.
And forgive us our trespasses
as we forgive those who trespass against us.
And lead us not into temptation
but deliver us from evil.
For thine is the kingdom,
the power and the glory.
For ever and ever. Amen.**

¶ PRAYERS OF PENITENCE

The Lord is full of gentleness and compassion.
In penitence and faith let us ask his forgiveness of our sins.

Kyrie from Missa Aeterna Christi munera by Giovanni Pierluigi da Palestrina
> *or*

Kyrie from Missa Orbis factor *(page 18)*
> *or*

English troped Kyrie by Andrew Reid *(page 20)*

Lord Jesus, you called us all to be one
yet we divide your Church to suit our own purposes.

Kyrie from Missa Aeterna Christi munera

Music: GIOVANNI PIERLUIGI DA PALESTRINA
(1525–1594)

Lord Jesus, you called the outcast to your side,
yet we cast out those whose views differ from our own.

Lord Jesus, you sent your Spirit to be the light and life of your Church, yet we have placed ourselves above the truth.

turn to page 23

Kyrie from Missa Orbis factor

Lord Jesus, you called us all to be one
yet we divide your Church to suit our own purposes.

OSSIA *(modern notation)*

Lord Jesus, you called the outcast to your side
yet we cast out those whose views differ from our own.

Lord Jesus, you sent your Spirit to be the light and life of your Church
yet we have placed ourselves above the truth.

CANTOR   ALL

Ky-ri- e   e-   le- i-son. Ky- ri- e   e-   le- i-son.

CANTOR

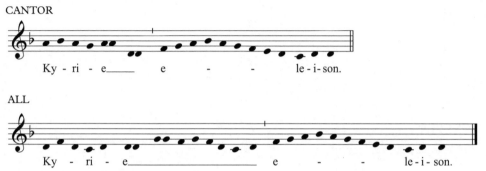

Ky - ri - e____   e   -   -   le - i- son.

ALL

Ky - ri - e_____   e   -   -   le - i- son.

turn to page 23

English troped Kyrie

Music: ANDREW REID

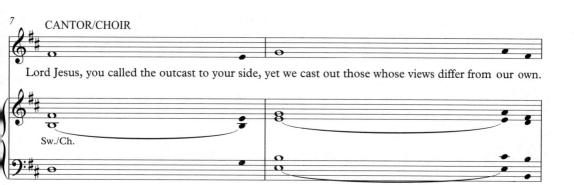

7

CANTOR/CHOIR

Lord Jesus, you called the outcast to your side, yet we cast out those whose views differ from our own.

Sw./Ch.

9

CANTOR/CHOIR   ALL

Christ,   have   mer - cy,   Christ   have   mer - cy.

Sw.   Gt

Ped.

13 CANTOR/CHOIR

Lord Jesus, you sent your Spirit to be the light and life of your Church,

Sw./Ch.

14

yet we have placed ourselves above the truth:

15 CANTOR/CHOIR   ALL

Lord,   have   mer - cy,   Lord   have   mer - cy.

Sw.

Gt

turn to next page

May the Father of all mercies
cleanse you from your sins,
and restore you in his image
to the praise and glory of his name,
through Jesus Christ our Lord.

All   **Amen.**

¶ THE WORD OF GOD

Canticle: A setting of Jubilate Deo (Psalm 100)

   Weelkes: Short Service *(page 24)*
        or
   Stanford: Unison setting in D *(page 30)*
        or
   Mathias: Make a joyful noise *(page 36)*

Canticle: Jubilate Deo from the Short Service

Music: THOMAS WEELKES
(1576–1623)

turn to page 42

Canticle: Jubilate Deo in D for Unison Voices

Music: CHARLES VILLIERS STANFORD
(1852–1924)

36

cresc.

way in-to his gates with thanks-giv-ing, and in-to his courts with praise:____

cresc.

42

f

____ be thank-ful un-to him, and speak good

f

48

of his Name. For the Lord___ is gra -

- cious, his mer - cy is ev - er - last - ing: and his

truth_____ en - dur-eth from ge - - ne - ra - tion to___

ge - - ne - ra - - - - - tion.

Glo - ry be to the Fa - ther, and to the Son:____ and to the

Ho - ly Ghost:_____ As it was in the be - gin - ning, is____

now, and ev - er shall_____ be:

turn to page 42

Canticle: Make a joyful noise (Psalm 100)

Music: WILLIAM MATHIAS
(1934–1992)

glad - ness;_____   come be-fore his pres-ence with sing - ing.

Know   ye__ that the Lord   he____ is   God:_____   Know   ye__ that the

Lord   he____ is   God:_____   it   is   he   that hath

poco a poco dim.

poco a poco dim.

made us,   and   not__ we__ our - selves:_____   it   is

he   that hath__ made us   and   not__ we__ our - selves:_____

we are his peo - ple,   and the   sheep   of his pas - ture.__

Ped.

-dur - eth to all ge - ne - ra - tions.

A - men, A-

Man.

- men, A - men.

turn to next page

Collect

Heavenly Father,
you have called us in the Body of your Son Jesus Christ
to continue his work of reconciliation
and reveal you to the world:
forgive us the sins which tear us apart;
give us the courage to overcome our fears
and to seek that unity which is your gift and your will;
through Jesus Christ your Son our Lord,
who is alive and reigns with you,
in the unity of the Holy Spirit,
one God, now and for ever.

All   Amen.

Old Testament Reading: Ezekiel 36. 23–28

I will sanctify my great name, which has been profaned among the nations, and which you have profaned among them; and the nations shall know that I am the Lord, says the Lord God, when through you I display my holiness before their eyes. I will take you from the nations, and gather you from all the countries, and bring you into your own land. I will sprinkle clean water upon you, and you shall be clean from all your uncleannesses, and from all your idols I will cleanse you. A new heart I will give you, and a new spirit I will put within you; and I will remove from your body the heart of stone and give you a heart of flesh. I will put my spirit within you, and make you follow my statutes and be careful to observe my ordinances. Then you shall live in the land that I gave to your ancestors; and you shall be my people, and I will be your God.

Psalm 122 – set to Anglican chant;

George J. Elvey

f 1   I was glad when they / said un·to / me:
         We will / go in·to the / house of · the / <u>Lord</u>.

2   Our / feet shall / stand // in thy / gates-- / O Je / rusalem.

mf 3   Jerusalem is / built · as a / city:
         that is at / uni·ty / in it / <u>self</u>.

4   For thither the tribes go up★,
         even the / tribes of · the / Lord:
     to testify unto Israel★,
         to give / thanks un · to the / Name of · the / Lord.

2nd 5   For there is the / seat of / judgement:
part   even the / seat of · the / house of / David.

p 6   O pray for the / peace of · Je- / rusalem:
         they shall / pros-- / per that / love thee.

7   Peace be with / in thy / walls:
         and / plenteousness · with / in thy / palaces.

mp 8   For my brethren and com- / panions' / sakes:
         I will / wish-- / thee pros- / peri · ty.

mf 9   Yea because of the house of the / Lord our / God:
         I will / seek to / do thee / good.

f   Glory / be · to the / Father:
         and to the Son★
         / and · to the / Holy / <u>Ghost</u>:
     as it was in the beginning★,
         is now and / ever / shall be:
         world without / end. A / --- / men.

Underlinings refer to a slight lengthening of a syllable to allow for the altos to sing two notes.

For Choral Evensong, turn to page 112

turn to page 49

Psalm 122 – tone iv;

Cantor	1	*I re*joiced / when they said to me :
I		"Let us go to the house of the / LORD."

II	2	And now our / feet are standing :
		within your gates, O Jeru / salem.

I	3	Jerusalem is built / as a city :
		bonded as one toge / ther.

II	4	It is there that the tribes go up, the / tribes of the LORD :
		For Israel's witness it is to praise the name of the / LORD.

I	5	There were set the / thrones for judgment :
		the thrones of the house of Da / vid.

II	6	For the peace of Je / rusalem pray :
		"May they prosper, those who love / you."

I	7	May peace abide / in your walls :
		and security be in your tow / ers.

II	8	For the sake of my / family and friends :
		let me say, "Peace upon / you."

I	9	For the sake of the house / of the LORD, our God :
		I will seek good things / for you.

II		Glory be to the Fa / ther and to the Son :
		and to the Holy Spi / rit.

I		As it was in the beginning, is now and / ever shall be :
		world without end. A / men.

This can be sung in one of several ways: The Cantor may start, with his/her group completing verse 1, followed by the alternate group in verse 2, etc.; Groups could be upper and lower voices; sides of the choir; Cantor versus full voices; Cantor-led small group versus remainder of choir and congregation.

turn to page 49

Anthem: Pray that Jerusalem

Words: Psalm 122
Scottish Psalter (1650)

Music: *melody from* Playford's Psalms (1671)
arranged by CHARLES VILLIERS STANFORD
(1852–1924)

love thee and thy peace have still pro-spe-ri - ty.

p *poco cresc.*

TENORS and BASSES

mf

There - fore I wish that peace may still with - in thy walls re-

p *mf*

main,   And   ev - er may thy pa - la - ces

cresc.

cresc.

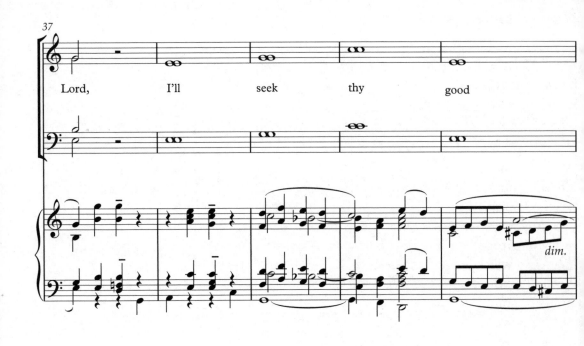

Lord,   I'll   seek   thy   good

al - - way.

Continue to next page

New Testament Reading: Colossians 3. 9–17

Do not lie to one another, seeing that you have stripped off the old self with its practices and have clothed yourselves with the new self, which is being renewed in knowledge according to the image of its creator. In that renewal there is no longer Greek and Jew, circumcised and uncircumcised, barbarian, Scythian, slave and free; but Christ is all and in all!

As God's chosen ones, holy and beloved, clothe yourselves with compassion, kindness, humility, meekness, and patience. Bear with one another and, if anyone has a complaint against another, forgive each other; just as the Lord has forgiven you, so you also must forgive. Above all, clothe yourselves with love, which binds everything together in perfect harmony. And let the peace of Christ rule in your hearts, to which indeed you were called in the one body. And be thankful. Let the word of Christ dwell in you richly; teach and admonish one another in all wisdom; and with gratitude in your hearts sing psalms, hymns, and spiritual songs to God. And whatever you do, in word or deed, do everything in the name of the Lord Jesus, giving thanks to God the Father through him.

Hymn

O worship the Lord in the beauty of holiness *(page 50)*
  or
Holy Spirit, living breath of God *(page 52)*

Hymn: O worship the Lord in the beauty of holiness

WAS LEBET   13 10 13 10

Music: Melody from *Rheinhardt MS*, 1754

1 O worship the Lord in the beauty of holiness!
    bow down before him, his glory proclaim;
  with gold of obedience, and incense of lowliness,
    kneel and adore him, the Lord is his name!

2 Low at his feet lay thy burden of carefulness,
    high on his heart he will bear it for thee,
  comfort thy sorrows, and answer thy prayerfulness,
    guiding thy steps as may best for thee be.

3 Fear not to enter his courts in the slenderness
    of the poor wealth thou wouldst reckon as thine:
  truth in its beauty, and love in its tenderness,
    these are the offerings to lay on his shrine.

4 These, though we bring them in trembling and fearfulness,
    he will accept for the name that is dear;
  mornings of joy give for evenings of tearfulness,
    trust for our trembling and hope for our fear.

5 O worship the Lord in the beauty of holiness!
    bow down before him, his glory proclaim;
  with gold of obedience, and incense of lowliness,
    kneel and adore him, the Lord is his name!

JOHN SAMUEL BEWLEY MONSELL (1811–1875)

turn to page 59

Hymn: Holy Spirit, living breath of God

Words and Music: KEITH GETTY (*b.* 1974) *and* STUART TOWNEND (*b.* 1963)
arranged by ANDREW REID

1. Ho - ly Spi- rit, liv-ing breath of God, breathe new life in - to my will- ing soul. Bring the pre -sence of the ri - sen Lord to re- -new my heart and make me whole. Cause your word to come a -

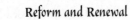

-live in me; give me faith for what I can-not see,

give me pas-sion for your pu – ri – ty; Ho - ly Spi - rit, breathe new life in

me.

and the least,___ gen - tle - ness that sows the path of peace.___

Turn my stri-vings in - to works of grace; Breath of God, show Christ in all I

do.___

DESCANT

Ho - ly Spi-rit from cre-

MELODY

Ho - ly Spi-rit from cre-

-a - tion's birth, giv-ing life to all that God has made,_

-a - tion's birth, giv-ing life to all that God has made,

show your pow-er once a - gain on Earth, cause your church to hun - ger

show your pow-er once a - gain on Earth, cause your church to hun-ger for your

for your ways___ May the fra-grance of our prayers a - rise;___

ways   May the fra-grance of our prayers a - rise;

lead us on the road of sa - cri - fice, that in u - ni - ty the

lead us on the road of sa - cri - fice, that in u - ni - ty the

face of Christ may be clear for all the world to see.

face of Christ may be clear for all the world to see.

Continue to next page

Address

Anthem

Bairstow: Though I speak with the tongues of men *(page 60)*
   or
Ireland: Greater Love *(page 71)*
   or
Shephard: Let the word of Christ *(page 84)*

Anthem: Though I speak with the tongues of men

1 Corinthians xiii. 1–4, 7–9, 12 and 13

Music: EDWARD CUTHBERT BAIRSTOW
(1874–1946)

it pro - fit-eth me no - thing.

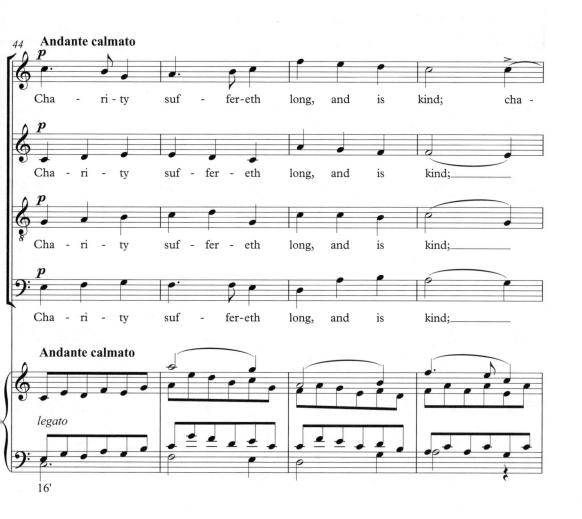

Cha - ri - ty suf - fer-eth long, and is kind; cha -

Cha - ri - ty suf - fer - eth long, and is kind;____

Cha - ri - ty suf - fer - eth long, and is kind;____

Cha - ri - ty suf - fer-eth long, and is kind;____

hop-eth all   things, en - dur - eth   all___ things.

things,   hop-eth all   things, en-dur - eth   all   things.

things,___   en - dur - eth   all   things.

things,   hop-eth all   things,   en-dur-eth all   things.

Cha - ri - ty   ne - ver   fail - eth:

but whe - ther there be pro - phe- cies, they shall fail: whe - ther

there be tongues, they shall cease: or   whe - ther there be know- ledge,

it shall van - ish___ a - way.

Man.

98

mf

And now a - bid - eth faith, hope and cha - ri - ty,

mf

Largamente

103

f *ff*

but the great - est of these is cha - ri - ty,

f *ff*

Largamente

f *ff*

108 *dim.* *pp*

cha - ri - ty, cha - ri - ty.

dim. *pp*

ppp

For Choral Evensong, turn to page 130

turn to page 96

Anthem: Greater love

Music: JOHN IRELAND
(1879–1962)

SOLO TREBLE

Who His own Self bare our sins in His own Bo-dy on the tree, that we be-ing dead____ to sins,___ should

SOLO BARITONE

live un-to right-eous-ness, that we be-ing dead____ to

friends.

friends.

friends.

friends.

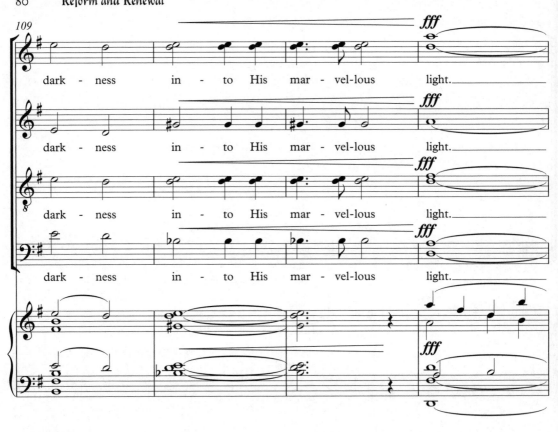

dark - ness   in - to His mar - vel-lous   light.

dark - ness   in - to His mar - vel-lous   light.

dark - ness   in - to His mar - vel-lous   light.

dark - ness   in - to His mar - vel-lous   light.

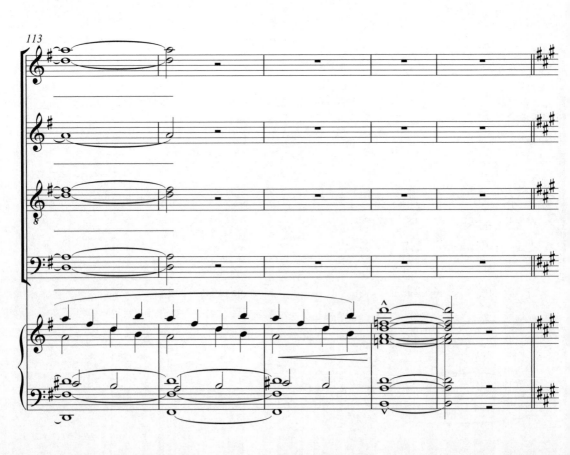

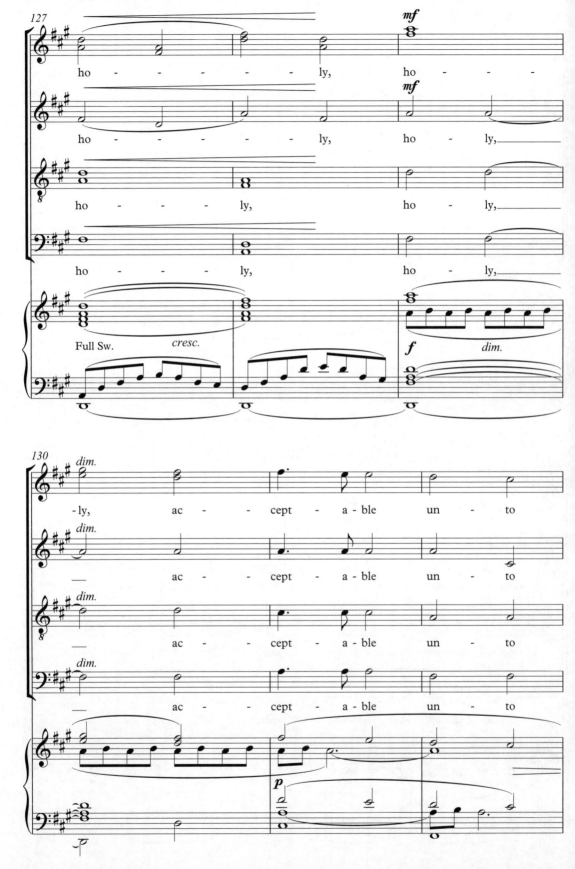

For Choral Evensong, turn to page 130

turn to page 96

Anthem: Let the word of Christ

Words: Colossians 3. 16–17
George Wither (1588–1667)

Music: RICHARD SHEPHARD
(b. 1949)

Ped.

in psalms and hymns____ and spi - ri - tu - al songs

sing - ing with grace in your hearts to the Lord

(unaccompanied ad. lib)   Man.

Sing-ing with grace in your hearts to___ the Lord.

Let the word___ of Christ dwell in you rich - ly in all wis - dom

Ped.

Let the word of Christ dwell in you rich - ly in all wis - dom.

And what - so - ev - er ye do in word or deed, do

Man.

Ped.

all in the name of the Lord_____ Je - sus,

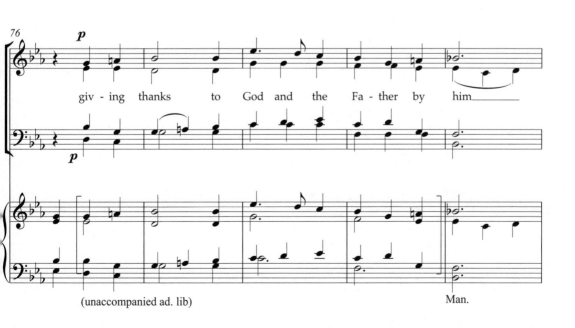

giv - ing thanks to God and the Fa - ther by him_____

(unaccompanied ad. lib)

Man.

And what - so - ev - er ye do in word or deed, do all in the

And what - so - ev - er ye do in word or deed, do

name of the Lord_____ Je - sus

all in the name of the Lord_____ Je - sus

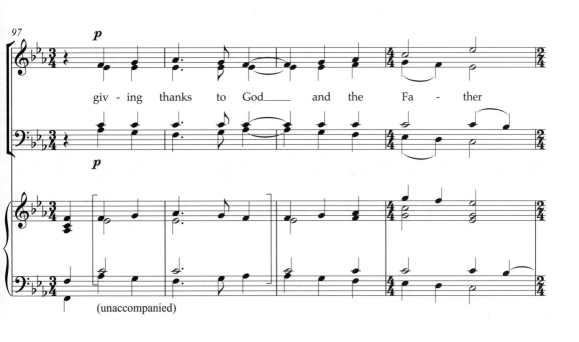

giv - ing   thanks   to   God____   and   the   Fa - ther

(unaccompanied)

poco rit. _ _ _ _ _ _ _ _ _ _

by   him.

Come, O come in pi - ous lays,__ Sound we God Al - migh-ty's praise;

Hi - ther bring, in one con-sent Heart and voice and in-stru - ment.

Let those things which do not live__ in still mu - sic prais - es give;

Not a__ crea - ture dumb be found,__ That hath ei - ther voice_ or sound.

And as-cend from sphere to sphere To the great Al - might- y's__ ear;

Then, O__ come, in pi - ous lays Sound we__ God Al -

rit al fine

migh - ty's praise. A - - men.

For Choral Evensong, turn to page 130

turn to next page

¶ THE REFORMING CHURCH

Reading – Anglicanism
From the Preface to the Book of Common Prayer, 1549

> Of such Ceremonies as be used in the Church, and have had their beginning
> by the institution of man, some at the first were of godly intent and purpose
> devised, and yet at length turned to vanity and superstition: some entered
> into the Church by undiscreet devotion, and such a zeal as was without
> knowledge; and for because they were winked at in the beginning, they grew
> daily to more and more abuses, which not only for their unprofitableness,
> but also because they have much blinded the people, and obscured the glory
> of God, are worthy to be cut away, and clean rejected: other there be, which
> although they have been devised by man, yet it is thought good to reserve
> them still, as well for a decent order in the Church, (for the which they were
> first devised) as because they pertain to edification, whereunto all things
> done in the Church (as the Apostle teacheth) ought to be referred.

Reading – Non-Conformism

> On May 24th, 1738 John Wesley opened his Bible at about five in the
> morning and came across these words, 'There are given unto us exceeding
> great and precious promises, even that ye should be partakers of the divine
> nature.' He read similar words in other places. That evening he reluctantly
> attended a meeting in Aldersgate. Someone read from Luther's Preface
> to the Epistle to Romans. About 8.45 p.m. 'while he was describing the
> change which God works in the heart through faith in Christ, I felt my heart
> strangely warmed. I felt I did trust in Christ, Christ alone for salvation; and
> an assurance was given me that He had taken away my sins, even mine, and
> saved me from the law of sin and death.'

Hymn – Evangelical Revival

And can it be *(page 98)*
> *or*
To God be the glory *(page 100)*

Hymn: And can it be

SAGINA   88 88 88 extended

1 And can it be that I should gain
        An interest in the Saviour's blood?
    Died he for me, who caused his pain?
        For me, who him to death pursued?
    Amazing love! How can it be
    That thou, my God, shouldst die for me?

2 'Tis mystery all : th' Immortal dies!
        Who can explore his strange design?
    In vain the first-born seraph tries
        To sound the depths of love divine.
    'Tis mercy all! Let earth adore,
    Let angel minds enquire no more.

3 He left his Father's throne above –
        So free, so infinite his grace –
    Emptied himself of all but love,
        And bled for Adam's helpless race.
    'Tis mercy all, immense and free;
    For, O my God, it found out me!

4 Long my imprisoned spirit lay
        Fast bound in sin and nature's night;
    Thine eye diffused a quickening ray –
        I woke, the dungeon flamed with light,
    My chains fell off, my heart was free,
    I rose, went forth, and followed thee.

5 No condemnation now I dread;
        Jesus, and all in him, is mine!
    Alive in him, my living head,
        And clothed in righteousness divine,
    Bold I approach th' eternal throne,
    And claim the crown, through Christ, my own.

CHARLES WESLEY (1707-1788)

The last two lines of each verse are repeated.

Music: from Thomas Campbell *The Bouquet*, 1825

turn to page 102

Hymn: To God be the glory

TO GOD BE THE GLORY   11 11 11 11 and refrain

1 To God be the glory, great things he has done!
   So loved he the world that he gave us his Son,
   Who yielded his life an atonement for sin,
   and opened the life-gate that all may go in:

   Praise the Lord! Praise the Lord!
   * Let the earth hear his voice!*
   Praise the Lord! Praise the Lord!
   * Let the people rejoice!*
   O come to the Father, through Jesus the Son;
   And give him the glory—great things he has done!

2 O perfect redemption, the purchase of blood,
   To every believer the promise of God!
   The vilest offender who truly believes,
   That moment from Jesus a pardon receives:
   Chorus

3 Great things he has taught us, great things he has done,
   And great our rejoicing through Jesus the Son;
   But purer, and higher, and greater will be
   Our wonder, our rapture, when Jesus we see:
   Chorus

FRANCES JANE VAN ALSTYNE (FANNY CROSBY) (1820–1915)

Music: GEORGE WASHINGTON DOANE (1799–1859)

turn to next page

Reading – Roman Catholic Reform

From Constitution of the Sacred Liturgy of the Second Vatican Council, 1963

Mother Church earnestly desires that all the faithful should be led to that fully conscious and active participation in liturgical celebrations which is demanded by the very nature of the liturgy. Such participation by the Christian people as 'a chosen race, a royal priesthood, a holy nation, a redeemed people', is their right and duty by reason of their baptism.

In the restoration and promotion of the sacred liturgy, this full and active participation by all the people is the aim to be considered before all else; for it is the primary and indispensable source from which the faithful are to derive the true Christian spirit; and therefore pastors of souls must zealously strive to achieve it, by means of the necessary instruction, in all their pastoral work.

[Yet it would be futile to entertain any hopes of realizing this unless the pastors themselves, in the first place, become thoroughly imbued with the spirit and power of the liturgy, and undertake to give instruction about it. A prime need, therefore, is that attention be directed, first of all, to the liturgical instruction of the clergy.]

¶ PRAYERS OF INTERCESSION

Words: Michael Hampel

Music: MARGARET RIZZA
(*b.* 1929)

(♩ = c.52)

With optional MELODY INSTRUMENT throughout

Man.
Optional CELLO

Prayer Leader *(spoken)*: We pray that Christ may be seen in the life of the Church.

p (background for spoken prayers)

Jesus, Lord of the Church

In   your   mer - cy,   hear   us.

You have called us into the family of those who are the children of God.

May our love for our brothers and sisters be strengthened by your grace.

Jesus, Lord of the Church

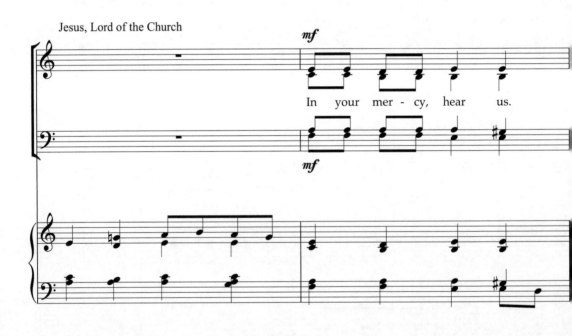

In your mer - cy, hear us.

You have called us to be a temple where the Holy Spirit can dwell.

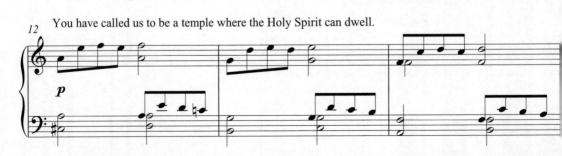

Give us clean hands and pure hearts, so that our lives will reflect your holiness.

Jesus, Lord of the Church

You have called us to be a light in the world, so that those in darkness come to you.

May our lives shine as a witness to the saving grace you have given for all.

Jesus, Lord of the Church

In   your   mer - cy,   hear   us.

25   You have called us to be members of your body, so that when one suffers, all suffer together.

28   We ask for your comfort and healing power to bring hope to those in distress.

Jesus, Lord of the Church

In   your   mer - cy,   hear   us.

You have called us to be the bride, where you, Lord, are the Bridegroom.

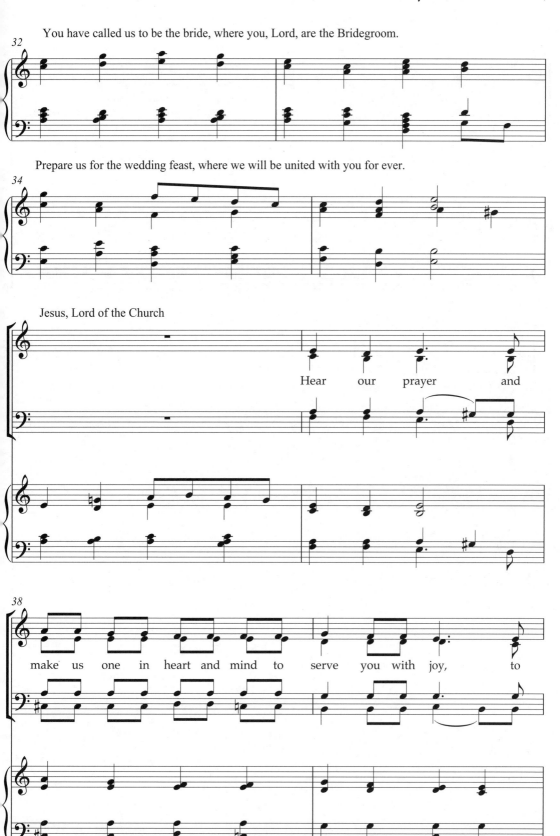

Prepare us for the wedding feast, where we will be united with you for ever.

Jesus, Lord of the Church

Hear our prayer and

make us one in heart and mind to serve you with joy, to

serve you with joy, with joy____ for e - ver, with joy____ for e - ver.

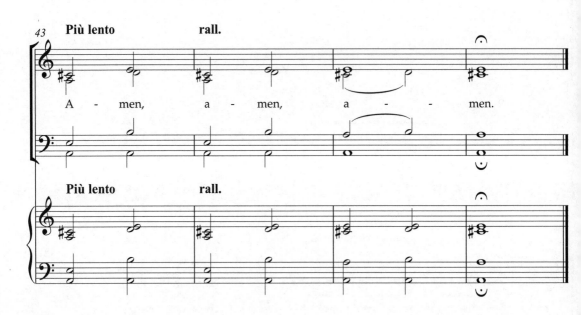

A - men, a - men, a - men.

Hymn

Now, from the heavens descending *(page 110)*
or
Lord of the Church, we pray for your renewing *(page 112)*

Hymn: Now, from the heavens descending

Music: Adapted from JOHANN CRÜGER (1598–1662)
            by WILLIAM HENRY MONK (1823–1889)

1 Now, from the heavens descending,
  is seen a glorious light,
the Bride of Christ in splendour,
  arrayed in purest white.
She is the Holy City,
  whose radiance is the grace
of all the saints in glory,
  from every time and place.

2 This is the hour of gladness
  for Bridegroom and for Bride;
the Lamb's great feast is ready;
  his Bride is at his side.
How bless'd are those invited
  to share his wedding-feast:
the least become the greatest,
  the greatest are the least.

3 He who is throned in heaven
  takes up his dwelling-place
among his chosen people
  who see him face to face.
No sound is heard of weeping,
  for pain and sorrow cease,
and sin shall reign no longer,
  but love and joy and peace.

4 See how a new creation
  is brought at last to birth,
a new and glorious heaven,
  a new and glorious earth.
Death's power for ever broken,
  its empire swept away,
the promised dawn of glory,
  begins its endless day.

JAMES QUINN S.J. (1919–2010)

turn to page 114

Hymn: Lord of the Church, we pray for our renewing

LONDONDERRY AIR   11 10 11 10 D

1 Lord of the church, we pray for our renewing:
       Christ over all, our undivided aim.
   Fire of the Spirit, burn for our enduing,
       wind of the Spirit, fan the living flame!
   We turn to Christ amid our fear and failing,
       the will that lacks the courage to be free,
   the weary labours, all but unavailing,
       to bring us nearer what a church should be.

2 Lord of the church, we seek a Father's blessing,
       a true repentance and a faith restored,
   a swift obedience and a new possessing,
       filled with the Holy Spirit of the Lord!
   We turn to Christ from all our restless striving,
       unnumbered voices with a single prayer:
   the living water for our souls' reviving,
       in Christ to live, and love and serve and care.

3 Lord of the church, we long for our uniting,
       true to one calling, by one vision stirred;
   one cross proclaiming and one creed reciting,
       one in the truth of Jesus and his word!
   So lead us on; till toil and trouble ended,
       one church triumphant one new song shall sing,
   to praise his glory, risen and ascended,
       Christ over all, the everlasting King!

TIMOTHY DUDLEY-SMITH (b. 1926)

Music: *Air from County Derry* from
         Irish Music as noted by George Petrie, 1903
         Harmonised by DONALD DAVISON (b. 1937)

For Choral Evensong, turn to page 142

turn to page 114

An Act of Commitment

Behold how good and pleasant it is
All   to dwell together in unity.

Let us commit ourselves anew
All   to be partners in the Gospel of Christ.

That we may be open to the prompting of the Spirit,
All   we make our promise to you, O Lord.

That we may continually build up the Body of Christ,
All   we make our promise to you, O Lord.

That we may pursue unity in diversity,
All   we make our promise to you, O Lord.

Lord Jesus Christ,
who said to your apostles,
'Peace I leave with you, my peace I give to you':
look not on our sins but on the faith of your Church
and grant it the peace and unity of your kingdom;
where you are alive and reign with the Father
in the unity of the Holy Spirit,
one God, now and for ever.
All   Amen.

[Presentation of awards]

¶ THE SENDING OUT

The Peace

We are all one in Christ Jesus.
We belong to him through faith,
Heirs of the promise of the Spirit of peace.

The peace of the Lord be always with you
All　**and also with you.**

Let us offer one another a sign of peace.

All may share a sign of peace with each other.

Anthem

Gjeilo: Ubi caritas *(page 116)*
　　or
Nardone: I give to you a new commandment *(page 122)*
　　or
Song: The peace of the earth *(page 127)*

Anthem: Ubi Caritas

Music: OLA GJEILO
(b. 1978)

et ex cor-de di - li - ga-mus nos sin-ce - ro._____

et ex cor-de di - li - ga-mus nos sin-ce - ro._____

et ex cor-de di - li - ga-mus nos sin-ce - ro._____

et ex cor-de di - li - ga-mus nos sin-ce - ro._____

U - bi ca - ri-tas et a - mor,____ De-us i - bi est. Con-gre-

U - bi ca - ri-tas et a - mor,____ De-us i - bi est. Con-gre-

U - bi ca - ri-tas et a - mor,____ De-us i - bi est. Con-gre-

ca-ri-tas et a - mor,____ De-us i - bi est. Con-gre-

turn to page 128

Anthem: I give to you a new commandment

Words: John 13. 34–35
and Liber Usualis

Music: PETER NARDONE
(*b.* 1965)

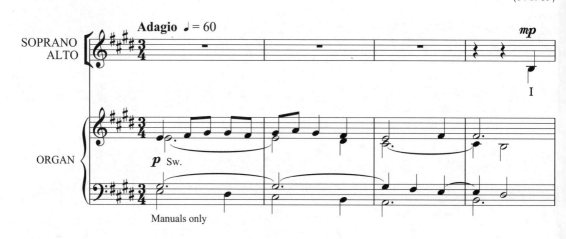

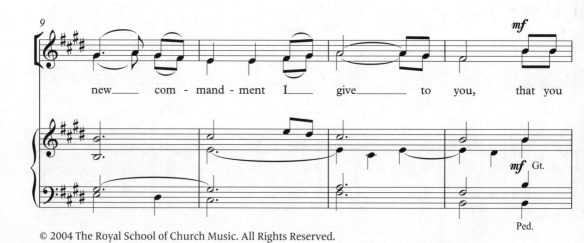

loved you, as I have loved you.

p I

et a -me - mus_ De-um vi - vum.

p

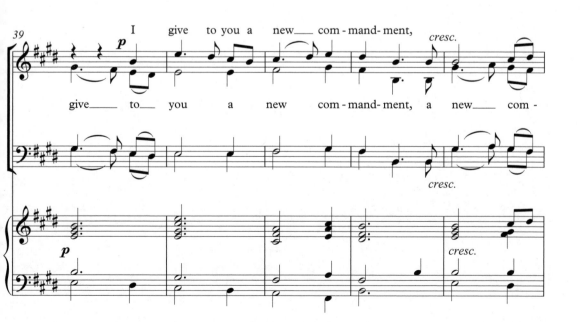

I give to you a new_ com - mand- ment, *cresc.*

give_ to_ you a new com -mand- ment, a new_ com -

p

cresc.

cresc.

turn to page 128

Song: The peace of the earth

Words: Guatemalan
translated by Christine Carson

Music: Guatemalan traditional song
arranged by GEOFF WEAVER

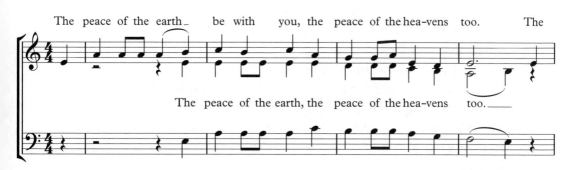

The peace of the earth be with you, the peace of the hea-vens too. The

The peace of the earth, the peace of the hea-vens too.

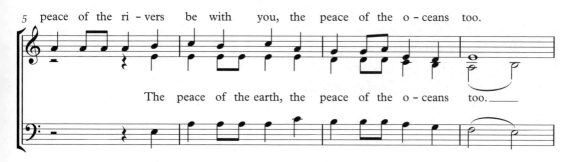

peace of the ri-vers be with you, the peace of the o-ceans too.

The peace of the earth, the peace of the o-ceans too.

Deep peace fall-ing o-ver you.

Deep peace fall-ing o-ver you.

Peace fall-ing o-ver you.

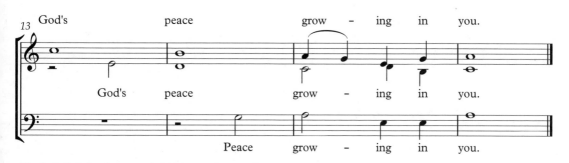

God's peace grow-ing in you.

God's peace grow-ing in you.

Peace grow-ing in you.

turn to next page

Blessing and Dismissal

The Lord Jesus Christ,
Son of the living God,
teach you to walk in his way more trustfully,
to accept his truth more faithfully,
and to share his life more lovingly;
that by the power of the Holy Spirit
you may come as one family to the kingdom of the Father.
And the blessing of God almighty,
the Father, the Son, and the Holy Spirit,
be among you and remain with you always.

All   Amen.

We go into the world
to walk in God's light,
to rejoice in God's love
and to reflect God's glory.

All   In the name of Christ, Amen.

Recessional Hymn

Church of God, elect and glorious *(page 130)*
    or
We have a gospel to proclaim *(page 134)*

Hymn: Church of God, elect and glorious

LUX EOI   87 87 D

Music: ARTHUR SEYMOUR SULLIVAN (1842–1900)
          descant by SIMON LOLE (*b.* 1957)

1 Church of God, elect and glorious,
       holy nation, chosen race;
   called as God's own special people,
       royal priests and heirs of grace:
   know the purpose of your calling,
       show to all his mighty deeds;
   tell of love which knows no limits,
       grace which meets all human needs.

2 God has called you out of darkness
       into his most marvellous light;
   brought his truth to life within you,
       turned your blindness into sight.
   Let your light so shine around you
       that God's name is glorified;
   and all find fresh hope and purpose
       in Christ Jesus crucified.

3 Once you were an alien people,
       strangers to God's heart of love;
   but he brought you home in mercy,
       citizens of heaven above.
   Let his love flow out to others,
       let them feel a Father's care;
   that they too may know his welcome
       and his countless blessings share.

turn over for last verse descant

4 Church of God, elect and holy,
       be the people he intends;
   strong in faith and swift to answer
       each command your master sends:
   royal priests, fulfil your calling
       through your sacrifice and prayer;
   give your lives in joyful service-
       sing his praise, his love declare.

JAMES E SEDDON (1915-1983)
FROM 1 PETER 2

DESCANT

4. Church of God, e - lect and ho - ly,   be the peo - ple he in - tends;

MELODY

4. Church of God, e - lect and ho - ly,   be the peo - ple he in - tends;

strong in   faith and   swift to an - swer each com - mand your mast - er sends:

strong   in faith   and   swift   to an - swer each com - mand your   mast - er sends:

ro - yal priests, ful - fil your   call - ing__ through your   sa - cri - fice;

roy-al priests, ful - fil   your call-ing through your   sa - cri - fice and prayer;

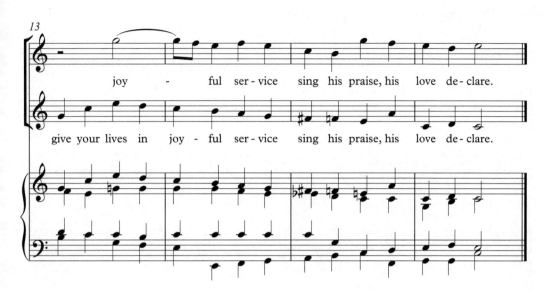

Hymn: We have a gospel to proclaim

FULDA   LM

Music: *Sacred Melodies*, 1815
          WILLIAM GARDINER (1770–1853)
          descant by ANDREW REID

1   We have a gospel to proclaim,
        good news for all throughout the earth;
    the gospel of a Saviour's name:
        we sing his glory, tell his worth.

2   Tell of his birth at Bethlehem
        not in a royal house or hall
    but in a stable dark and dim,
        the Word made flesh, a light for all.

3   Tell of his death at Calvary,
        hated by those he came to save,
    in lonely suffering on the Cross;
        for all he loved his life he gave.

UNISON   4   Tell of that glorious Easter morn:
        empty the tomb, for he was free.
    He broke the power of death and hell
        that we might share his victory.

5   Tell of his reign at God's right hand,
        by all creation glorified.
    He sends his Spirit on his Church
        to live for him, the Lamb who died.

turn over for last verse descant

6   Now we rejoice to name him King:
        Jesus is Lord of all the earth.
    This gospel-message we proclaim:
        we sing his glory, tell his worth.

EDWARD J BURNS (*b.* 1938)

DESCANT

6. Now we re - joice to name____ him King:

6. Now we re - joice to name__ him King:

Je - sus is Lord____ of all____ the earth.

Je - sus is Lord of all____ the earth. This

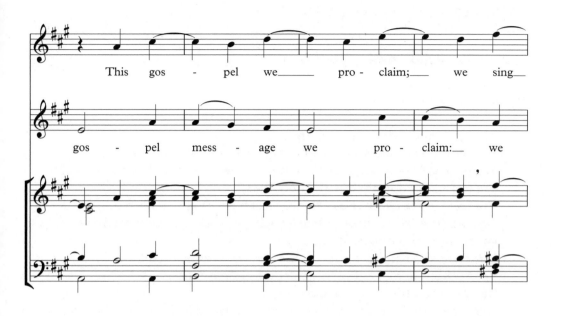

This gos - pel we___ pro - claim;___ we sing___

gos - pel mess - age we pro - claim:___ we

___ his glo - ry, tell___ his worth.

sing his glo - ry, tell___ his worth.

¶ ADDITIONAL CHORAL RESOURCES

Plainsong Versicles and Responses

The General Confession

All   **Almighty and most merciful Father,**
We have erred, and strayed from thy ways like lost sheep,
We have followed too much the devices and desires of our own hearts,
We have offended against thy holy laws,
We have left undone those things which we ought to have done,
And we have done those things which we ought not to have done,
And there is no health in us:
But thou, O Lord, have mercy upon us miserable offenders;
Spare thou them, O God, which confess their faults,
Restore thou them that are penitent,
According to thy promises declared unto mankind in Christ Jesu our Lord:
And grant, O most merciful Father, for his sake,
That we may hereafter live a godly, righteous, and sober life,
To the glory of thy holy Name.
Amen.

O Lord, open thou our lips. **And our mouth shall shew forth thy praise.**

O God, make speed to save us, **O Lord, make haste to help us.**

Glory be to the Father, and to the Son, and to the Ho - ly Ghost.

As it was in the beginning, is now, and ever shall be★, world without end.   A-men

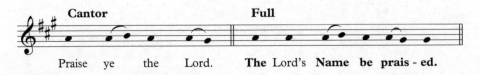

Praise ye the Lord.   **The Lord's Name be prais - ed.**

For Choral Evensong, turn to page 43

The Apostles' Creed

**I believe in God the Father Almighty,
Maker of heaven and earth:
And in Jesus Christ his only Son our Lord,
Who was conceived by the Holy Ghost,
Born of the Virgin Mary,
Suffered under Pontius Pilate,
Was crucified, dead, and buried:
He descended into hell;
The third day he rose again from the dead;
He ascended into heaven,
And sitteth on the right hand of God the Father Almighty;
From thence he shall come to judge the quick and the dead.
I believe in the Holy Ghost;
The holy Catholick Church;
The Communion of Saints;
The Forgiveness of sins;
The Resurrection of the body,
And the Life everlasting.
Amen.**

The Lord be with you. **And with thy spi - rit.**

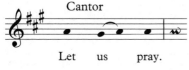

Let us pray.

Lord, have mercy up-on us. **Christ, have mercy up-on us.**

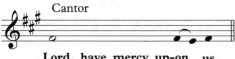

Lord, have mercy up-on us.

Our   Fa - ther:

Who art in heav'n
Hallowed be thy name;
Thy kingdom come;
Thy will be done;
On earth as it is in heav'n.
Give us this day our daily bread.
And forgive us our trespasses,
As we forgive those who trespass against us.

And lead us not into temptation,   but deliver us from evil.   A - men.

O Lord, shew thy mercy up - on   us.   **And grant us thy sal - va - tion.**

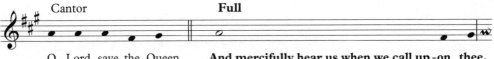

O Lord, save the Queen.   **And mercifully hear us when we call up - on   thee.**

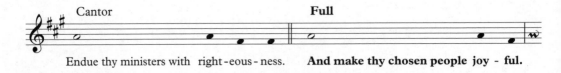

Endue thy ministers with right - eous - ness.   **And make thy chosen people joy - ful.**

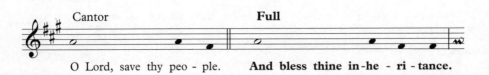

O Lord, save thy peo - ple.   **And bless thine in - he - ri - tance.**

Give peace in our time, O Lord. **Because there is none other**

that fight-eth for us,   but on - ly thou, O God.

O God, make clean our hearts with - in   us.   **And take not thy Holy Spirit from   us.**

Collect of the Day

Al-might-y God . . .   . . . now   and for ev - er.   **A - men.**

Collect for Peace

O God, from whom all holy desires...   Jesus Christ our   Sa - viour.   **A - men.**

Collect for aid against all perils

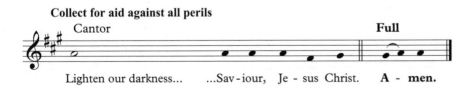

Lighten our darkness...   ...Sav - iour, Je - sus Christ.   **A - men.**

For Choral Evensong, turn to page 60, 71 or 84

For The Royal School of Church Music, 2016

The Sarum Service
Magnificat

Music: MALCOLM ARCHER
(b. 1953)

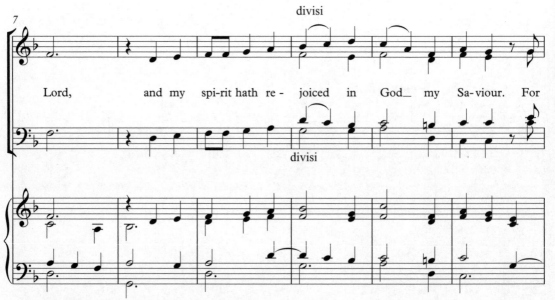

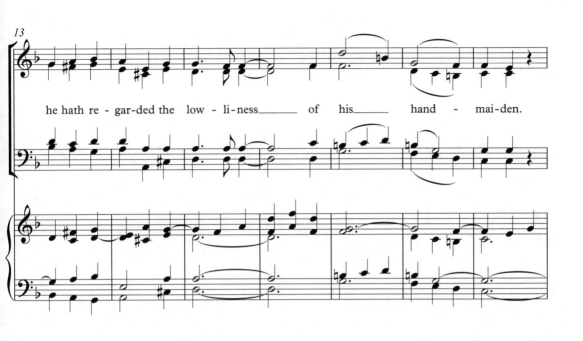

he hath re - gar-ded the low - li-ness_____ of his_____ hand - mai-den.

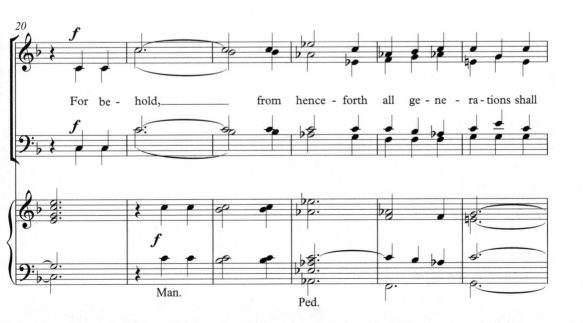

For be - hold,_____ from hence - forth all ge - ne - ra - tions shall

call   me   bles - sed.___   For   he   that   is   migh-ty   hath mag - ni-fi-ed

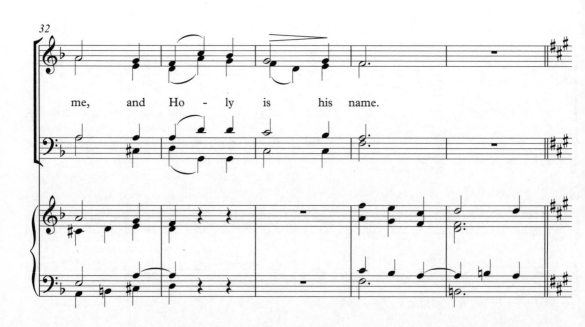

me,   and   Ho - ly   is   his   name.

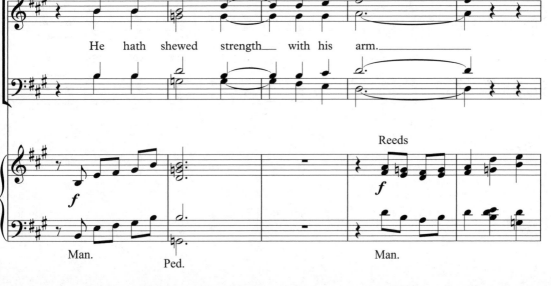

51

He hath scat-tered the proud in the im - a - gi - na - tion

55

of   their   hearts.   He   hath

Reeds

59

put down the migh - ty____ from their seat, and hath ex -

_mf_

Gt.

_mf_

Ped.

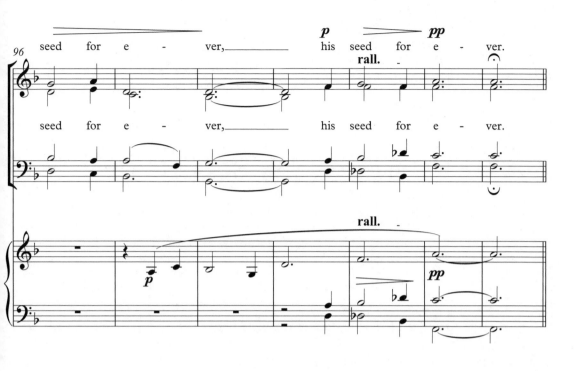

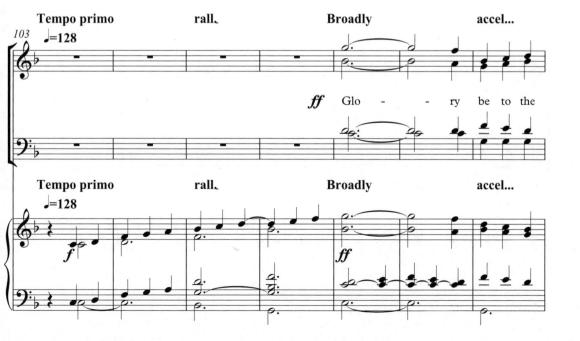

Fa-ther, and to the Son, and to the Hol - ly__ Ghost. As it

was in the be - gin - ning is now and e - ver shall be,

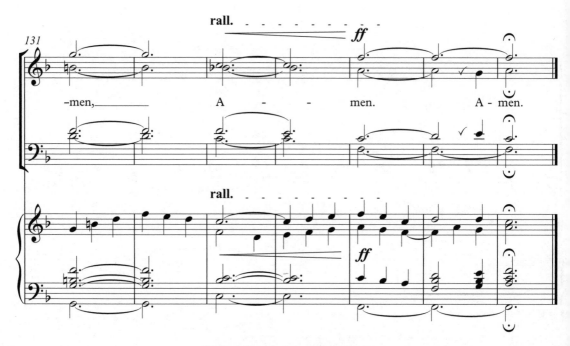

The Sarum Service
Nunc Dimittis

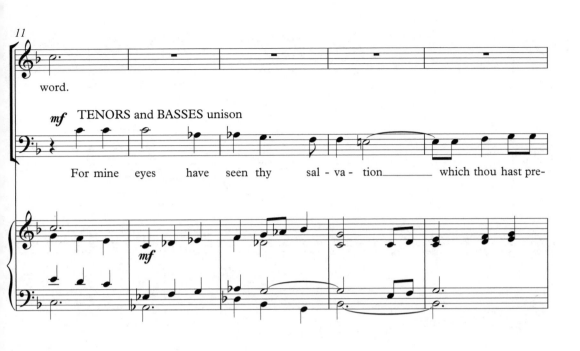

mf TENORS and BASSES unison

For mine eyes have seen thy sal - va - tion_____ which thou hast pre-

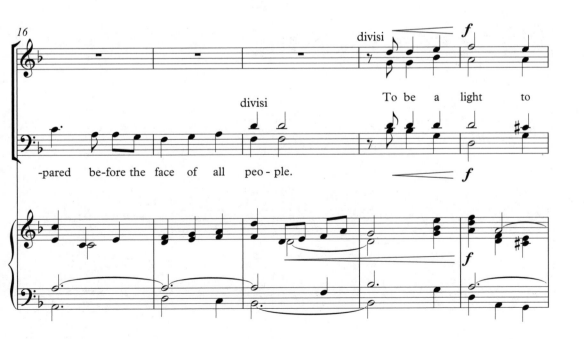

-pared be-fore the face of all peo - ple.

divisi

To be a light to

ligh-ten   the gen-tiles,   and to be the glo -   ry

of   thy_ peo - ple   Is - ra - el

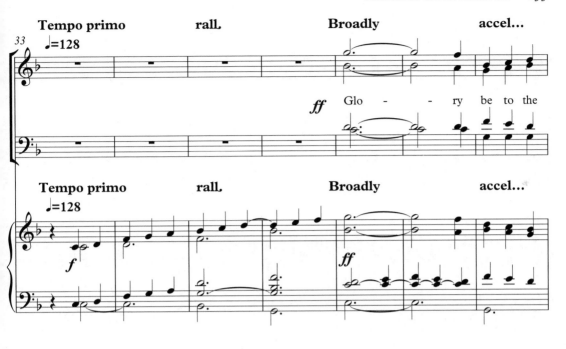

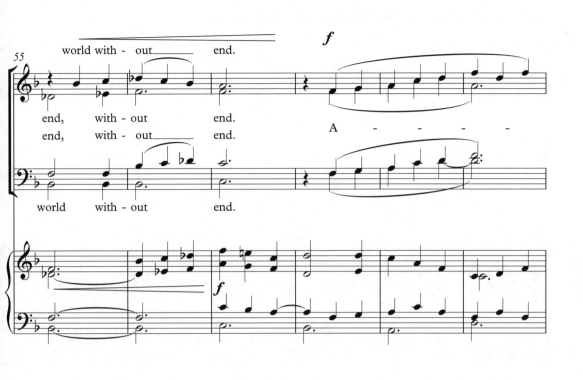

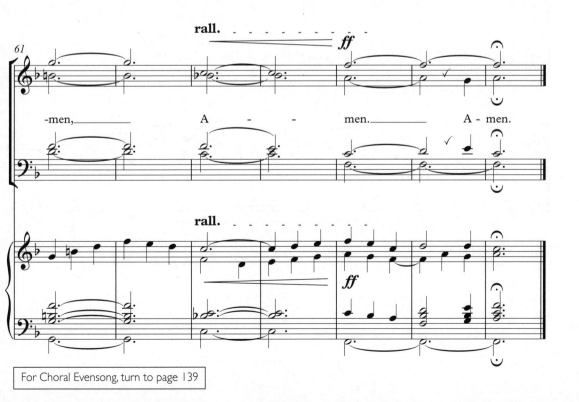

For Choral Evensong, turn to page 139

Accompaniment to Plainchant Kyrie (page 18)